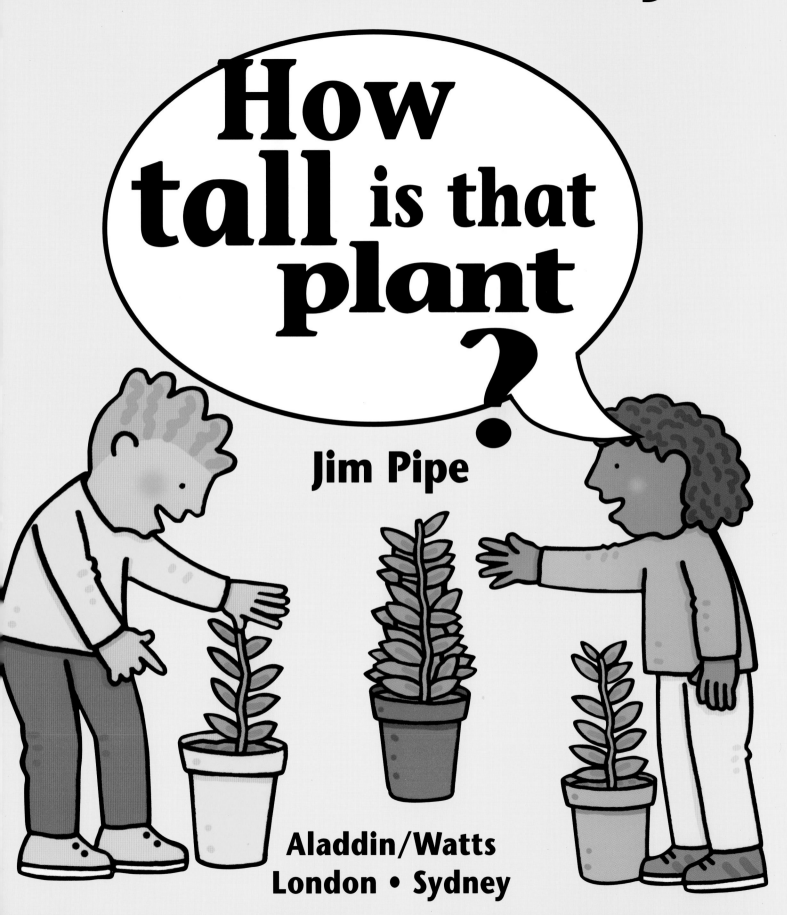

How tall is that plant?

Jim Pipe

Aladdin/Watts
London • Sydney

Which plant is the tallest?

Zack, Jo, Amy and Steve are growing bean plants in Jo's kitchen. They want to find out which plant is tallest.

Which plant is tallest? I think it is Jo's plant.

2

Let's see how the children find out.

3

We can also measure the plants using wall tiles. Steve's plant is as tall as four tiles.

Your plant is as high as five tiles, Jo, so it is the tallest!

Why it works

To compare the height or length of two or more objects, put them side by side. Then line them up so you measure them from the same point. Zack does this by putting all the plants on the floor. Don't look at how wide an object is as its shape can make it look shorter or taller than it really is. Other objects can help you compare sizes. Jo used wall tiles to measure the plants.

Solve the puzzle!

What can you measure with parts of your body? See how to use your hands and feet on page 22!

What can you use to measure things?

The children are playing in the garden with Steve's play people. When Amy sees Zack standing near the castle, he looks like a giant!

3

A play person is 12 centimetres tall. So 10 figures are 10 x 12 = 120 centimetres.

You're 115 centimetres tall. That's not quite as tall as ten figures.

4

Why it works

You can measure objects in your head by comparing them with something else. Steve looked at a play person then guessed how much taller Zack was. You can also measure things using another object. Amy measured Zack using play people. But to measure an object exactly, use a ruler or a tape measure. They show length in centimetres (cm) and metres (m).

Solve the puzzle

Look at an object near you. Can you guess how long or tall it is? Then check your guess by measuring the object with a ruler.

9

Who made the big, muddy footprint?

When the children come in from the garden, Steve and Zack forget to take off their shoes. Jo's dad is not very happy!

11

Let's see how the children find out.

Now let's count the squares, counting every two half squares as one square. Zack's foot covers 49 squares.

3

Steve's foot covers 52 squares, so Steve's foot *is* bigger.

Why it works

The "area" of an object is the size of its surface. So the area of a footprint is the surface covered by the bottom of a shoe or foot. The size of an area depends on both how long and how wide it is. So a long, thin object can have the same area as a short, wide object. Squared paper helps you to measure areas, even with an odd shape like a foot.

Solve the puzzle

Can you measure the area of your hand? Draw around it on squared paper, then count the squares.

13

Which holds the most water?

The children are helping Jo's dad to water the garden. They fill old jugs, pots and trays with water from the tap.

14

Let's see how the children find out.

If we pour the water into a measuring jug we can see exactly how much this jug holds.

3

You need to look at the marks on the side. Look, the jug holds about 1 litre.

Why it works

You can guess how much liquid something can hold by comparing it with an object you know well, like a cup. So when you see a bottle or a jug, think how many cups of water it can hold. To measure an amount of liquid exactly, use a measuring jug. This measures liquids in millilitres (ml) and litres (l).

Solve the puzzle

How much water can a balloon hold? Fill a balloon with water (not too much!). Then guess how many cups or litres of water it holds. How can you check your guess?

How many sweets?

The children are sharing out their sweets, which are all shapes and sizes. Jo likes toffees, Zack likes sticks of licorice, and Amy and Steve like mints. How can they share out the sweets fairly?

The sweets are different shapes and sizes, but they all weigh something.

This big sweet feels as heavy as six small ones.

18

19

Let's see how the children find out.

It takes 12 mints to make the elastic band stretch down to the toffee's mark.

So one toffee weighs as much as 12 tiny mints. If we weigh all the sweets like this, we can share them out fairly.

Why it works

It can be hard to guess an object's weight by looking at it. A quick way to guess is to pick it up in your hand. Amy compared the weight of different sweets like this. Scales are more exact. Jo's scales showed that 12 mints weighed as much as one toffee. Kitchen scales weigh things in grams (g) and kilograms (kg).

Solve the puzzle!

Pick up metal, wooden and plastic spoons that are the same size. Which feels heaviest? Now check by measuring their weight using a kitchen scales.

21

Did you solve the puzzles?

What can you measure with parts of your body?

People have always used their body to measure things. We still measure a horse's height in hands (one "hand" is 10 cm, the width of an adult hand). Measure a friend by putting one hand on top of the other from their head to their toes! You can measure a room by putting one foot in front of the other until you reach the far wall.

Can you guess how long or tall it is?

Like Zack, you can get better at guessing how tall or long something is by practising. Builders do this sort of quick guess all the time to work out how much wood or how many bricks they will need. Then they use a ruler or tape measure to check the exact measurement.

Can you measure the area of your hand?

If you draw around a hand or foot, you will find whole squares and parts of squares inside the shape. Count the whole squares, then add half squares, counting every 2 halves as 1 whole square.

How much water can a balloon hold?

Carefully pour the water from the balloon into a cup. How many cups of water does your balloon hold? Now, ask an adult to help you measure the water using a measuring jug. How many millilitres of water can your balloon hold?

Which feels heaviest?

Some materials are heavier than others. When you weigh the spoons, you should find the plastic spoon is lightest, then the wooden, and the metal spoon is heaviest. Did you guess correctly?

23

Index

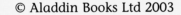

© Aladdin Books Ltd 2003

Designed and produced by
Aladdin Books Ltd
28 Percy Street
London W1T 2BZ

First published in
Great Britain in 2003 by
Franklin Watts
96 Leonard Street
London EC2A 4XD

ISBN 0 7496 4970 4

A catalogue record for this book is
available from the British Library.

Printed in U.A.E.

Literacy Consultant
Jackie Holderness
Westminster Institute of Education
Oxford Brookes University

Science Consultants
Helen Wilson and David Coates
Westminster Institute of Education
Oxford Brookes University

Science Tester
Alex Laar

Design
Flick, Book Design and Graphics

Illustration
Jo Moore